The Drop Shipping Blueprint

A Step-by-Step Guide to Building a Successful Online Business"

by:

Robert H. walker

Copyright© 2023 Robert h. Walker

All rights reserved

Table of Contents

Introduction

Welcome to "The Drop Shipping Blueprint: A Step-by-Step Guide to Building a Successful Online Business." In this book, you will learn everything you need to know about drop shipping and how to build a successful online business utilizing this e-commerce model.

Drop shipping is a retail fulfillment method where a store does not keep the products it sells in stock. Instead, when a store sells a product, it purchases the item from a third party and has it shipped directly to the customer. This eliminates the need for a store to keep large inventories of products on hand, reducing the overall cost of operating a business.

Not only does drop shipping offer a cost-effective solution for starting an online business, but it also provides a number of other benefits. It allows you to offer a wide range of products without the need for large investments, it enables you to test new products and market quickly, and it gives you more flexibility in terms of where and how you operate your business.

However, drop shipping is not without its challenges. Finding the right products to sell, building a reputable online store, and effectively marketing and advertising your business are just a few of the obstacles you may face. That is why this book is designed to be a comprehensive guide, walking you through each step of the process and providing you with the tools and resources you need to succeed.

Throughout this book, you will learn about researching demand, identifying and evaluating suppliers, building and optimizing your online store, creating a marketing plan, managing and scaling your business, and more. Whether you are a complete beginner or have some experience in e-commerce, this book will provide you with the knowledge and skills you need to build a profitable drop shipping business.

Let's get started!

What is Drop Shipping?

Drop shipping is a retail fulfillment method in which a store does not keep the products it sells in stock. Instead, when a store sells a product, it purchases the item from a third party supplier, often referred to as the drop shipper, and has it shipped directly to the customer. This eliminates the need for a store to keep large inventories of products on hand, reducing the overall cost of operating a business.

The process of drop shipping typically works as follows:

A customer places an order on the store's website.

The store sends the order and shipping details to the drop shipper.

The drop shipper ships the product directly to the customer.

The store keeps the difference between the retail price and the wholesale price as profit.

One of the main benefits of drop shipping is that it allows for a low barrier to entry for starting an online business. Since the store does not need to purchase and hold inventory, start-up costs can be significantly lower. Additionally, drop shipping allows the store to offer a wide range of products without the need for large investments. It also enables the store to test new products and market quickly, and give more flexibility in terms of where and how the store operates its business.

However, it is important to note that drop shipping also has its challenges. Finding the right products to sell, building a reputable online store, and effectively marketing and advertising the business are just a few of the obstacles that a business may face. It's also important to find reliable and trustworthy suppliers, as well as managing the shipping and customer service aspect of the business.

Overall, drop shipping can be a great way to start an online business, but it requires careful planning and execution to be successful. It is important to do proper research, understand the process and potential challenges before starting a drop shipping business.

Benefits of Drop Shipping

Drop shipping offers a number of benefits for those looking to start an online business. Some of the key benefits include:

Low Start-Up Costs: One of the main benefits of drop shipping is that it allows for a low barrier to entry for starting an online business. Since the store does not need to purchase and hold inventory, start-up costs can be significantly lower.

Wide Range of Products: Drop shipping allows the store to offer a wide range of products without the need for large investments. This can help attract more customers and increase sales.

Flexibility in Operations: Drop shipping gives the store more flexibility in terms of where and how it operates its business. It allows the store to test new products and market quickly, and to move the location of the store without having to worry about inventory storage.

Reduced Risk: Drop shipping allows the store to reduce the risk associated with traditional retail. Since the store does not need to purchase inventory upfront, it is not at risk of losing money on unsold products.

Scalability: Drop shipping allows the store to scale its business up or down as needed. As the store grows, it can increase the number of products it offers and expand into new markets.

Automation of Processes: Many drop shippers have an integrated system with their suppliers, which makes the process of ordering and shipping much more efficient and automated. This can save time and reduce the need for manual labor.

Reduced Overhead Costs: Since the store does not need to maintain a physical storefront or warehouse, overhead costs can be significantly reduced. This allows the store to invest more money into marketing and advertising efforts.

Increased Cash Flow: Drop shipping allows the store to increase cash flow by only paying for the products once they have been sold. This can help the store to grow more quickly and invest more money into the business.

While drop shipping has its benefits, it's important to understand and manage the challenges and risks that come with it, such as finding reliable suppliers, managing shipping and customer service and understanding the market trends and demands. It's important to do proper research, understand the process and potential challenges before starting a drop shipping business.

Potential Challenges

While drop shipping offers many benefits for those looking to start an online business, it also comes with a number of potential challenges that must be addressed to be successful. Some of the key challenges include:

Finding Reliable Suppliers: One of the biggest challenges of drop shipping is finding reliable and trustworthy suppliers. Since the supplier is responsible for shipping the products directly to the customer, it's crucial to work with suppliers that can provide good quality products and ship them on time.

Managing Shipping and Customer Service: As the store does not handle the shipping and handling of the products, it's important to have a clear communication and understanding with the supplier on how they handle these aspects. The store still needs to be able to provide good customer service and handle any issues that may arise.

Competition: Because drop shipping is a popular model, there is a lot of competition in the market. To be successful, the store needs to be able to differentiate itself and offer something unique to customers.

Margins: Since the store does not purchase the products at wholesale prices, the profit margins can be smaller than traditional retail. It's important to research and understand the market trends, prices and margins to make sure the business is profitable.

Quality Control: Since the store does not handle the products directly, it can be difficult to ensure the quality of the products. It's important to research and understand the supplier's quality control processes and to have a clear communication with the supplier on how to handle any issues that may arise.

Lack of Control: Since the store does not handle the products directly, it has less control over the entire process. This can make it more challenging to ensure that the products are shipped on time and to handle any issues that may arise.

Adapting to Market Trends: The market trends are constantly changing, and it's important to keep up with these changes and adapt accordingly. It's important to do proper research on the market trends, demands, and competition to make sure the business stays relevant.

Branding and Marketing: Without a physical storefront, it can be more challenging to establish a strong brand and attract customers. It's important to invest in branding and marketing efforts to build a strong online presence.

Overall, while drop shipping offers many benefits, it also comes with its own set of challenges. It's important to understand and manage these challenges to be successful in a drop shipping business. It's important to do proper research, understand the process and potential challenges before starting a drop shipping business.

Chapter one

Finding the Right Products

Finding the right products to sell is one of the most critical steps in building a successful drop shipping business. The products you choose will determine the success or failure of your business, so it's essential to invest the time and effort to find the right products to sell.

In this section, we will cover the following topics:

A. Researching Demand: The first step in finding the right products is to research demand. This involves identifying which products are in high demand, what the market trends are, and what kind of competition exists. By understanding demand, you can identify the products that are most likely to sell well.

B. Identifying Suppliers: Once you have identified the products you want to sell, the next step is to find suppliers that can provide those products. This involves researching different suppliers, evaluating their quality, and identifying the ones that are the most reliable and trustworthy.

C. Evaluating Quality: The quality of the products you sell is crucial to the success of your business. It's essential to evaluate the quality of the products and suppliers before making a decision. This includes researching the materials used, testing the products, and reading reviews.

D. Negotiating Prices: Once you have identified the right products and suppliers, the next step is to negotiate prices. This involves identifying the wholesale prices, determining the retail prices, and negotiating with suppliers to get the best possible prices.

By following these steps, you can find the right products to sell, identify reliable and trustworthy suppliers, and negotiate the best possible prices. By taking the time to find the right products, you can increase your chances of success and build a profitable drop shipping business.

It's important to note that, finding the right products to sell is an ongoing process and it's essential to stay updated with market trends, and customer demands. The store should also consider testing new products and diversify the products it offers as it grows.

Researching Demand

Researching demand is an essential step in finding the right products to sell in your drop shipping business. This involves identifying which products are in high demand, what the market trends are, and what kind of competition exists. By understanding demand, you can identify the products that are most likely to sell well.

Here are a few ways to research demand:

Analyze Sales Data: One of the best ways to research demand is by analyzing sales data. This includes looking at data on sales of similar products, identifying the products that are selling well, and understanding why they are selling well.

Use Market Research Tools: There are various market research tools available that can help you analyze demand, such as Google Trends, Amazon Best Sellers, and SEMrush. These tools can help you identify which products are in high demand, what the market trends are, and what kind of competition exists.

Conduct Surveys: Conducting surveys can be a great way to research demand. Surveys can be used to gather feedback from customers on what they are looking for in a product, what they are willing to pay, and what their pain points are.

Monitor Social Media: Social media can be a great way to research demand. By monitoring social media, you can identify which products are being talked about and which are trending. This can give you a good idea of what people are looking for and what they are willing to pay for.

Look at Competitors: Analyzing the products offered by your competitors can also provide valuable insights into what is in demand. By looking at the products that are selling well for your competitors, you can identify opportunities for your own business.

By researching demand, you can gain a better understanding of the products that are in high demand and what the market trends are. This information can help you make informed decisions about which products to sell, how to price them, and how to market them. It's important to note that researching demand is an ongoing process and it's essential to stay updated with market trends, and customer demands to adapt accordingly.

Identifying Suppliers

Once you have identified the products you want to sell through researching demand, the next step is to find suppliers that can provide those products. Identifying suppliers is a crucial step in building a successful drop shipping business, as the supplier is responsible for shipping the products directly to the customer. It's essential to find reliable and trustworthy suppliers to ensure that the products are of good quality, shipped on time and to handle any issues that may arise.

Here are a few ways to identify suppliers:

Online Marketplaces: Online marketplaces such as Alibaba and SaleHoo, connect retailers with a wide range of suppliers. These marketplaces allow you to search for suppliers by product category and filter results by location, price, and other criteria.

Wholesale Directories: Wholesale directories such as Worldwide Brands and Doba, list pre-vetted suppliers and provide access to thousands of products. These directories can be a great resource for finding suppliers that can provide the products you're looking for.

Trade Shows: Trade shows are a great way to meet suppliers in person and to see their products firsthand. This can be a great way to evaluate the quality of the products and the reliability of the suppliers.

Manufacturer Websites: Many manufacturers have their own websites where they list the products they offer and the prices. This can be a great way to find suppliers for specific products.

Referrals: Asking for referrals from other businesses can be a great way to find suppliers. This can help you to find suppliers that are reliable, trustworthy, and have a proven track record.

It's important to note that, it's essential to evaluate the supplier's quality and reliability before making a decision. This includes researching the supplier's reputation, reading reviews, and testing the products. Negotiating prices and creating a clear communication and understanding with the supplier on how they handle shipping and customer service is also important. By taking the time to identify reliable and trustworthy suppliers, you can increase your chances of success and build a profitable drop shipping business.

Evaluating Quality

Evaluating the quality of the products and suppliers is an essential step in building a successful drop shipping business. The quality of the products you sell is crucial to the success of your business, as it directly affects customer satisfaction and your brand reputation. Ensuring that the products you sell are of good quality can help to increase customer loyalty, reduce returns and negative reviews, and boost sales.

Here are a few ways to evaluate the quality of products and suppliers:

Research Materials Used: Researching the materials used to make the products is one of the first steps in evaluating quality. This can help you to identify the products that are made from high-quality materials, and which ones are made from cheaper, lower quality materials.

Test the Products: Testing the products can give you a good idea of their quality and performance. This can include assessing the product's durability, functionality, and overall design.

Read Reviews: Reading reviews from other customers can also be a great way to evaluate the quality of the products. This can help you to identify products that have a high level of customer satisfaction, as well as those that have a high number of negative reviews.

Evaluate the Supplier: Evaluating the supplier's quality and reliability is also crucial. This includes researching the supplier's reputation, reading reviews, and asking for references.

Evaluate the Packaging: Evaluating the packaging of the products can also be a way to evaluate the quality of the products. The packaging should be well-designed, sturdy and protect the product during shipping.

Check the Return Policy: Checking the supplier's return policy is also important. It's essential to work with suppliers that have a fair and flexible return policy.

By taking the time to evaluate the quality of the products and suppliers, you can ensure that you are selling high-quality products that will be well-received by customers. This can help to increase customer loyalty, reduce returns and negative reviews, and boost sales. It's important to note that, it's essential to regularly evaluate the quality of the products and suppliers to ensure that they meet your standards and customer's expectations.

Negotiating Prices

Negotiating prices with suppliers is an important step in building a successful drop shipping business. The prices you pay for products will directly impact your profits, so it's essential to negotiate the best possible prices with suppliers. By getting the best prices, you can increase your profits, making it easier to grow your business.

Here are a few tips for negotiating prices with suppliers:

Research Wholesale Prices: The first step in negotiating prices is to research the wholesale prices of the products you want to sell. This will give you a good idea of what the products should cost and will help you to identify suppliers that are offering good prices.

Determine Retail Prices: Once you have identified the wholesale prices, you'll need to determine the retail prices. This will help you to calculate the profit margins, and determine how much you need to charge to make a profit.

Identify Your Leverage: Identifying your leverage is important when negotiating prices. This includes understanding the supplier's competition, identifying the supplier's needs, and identifying any products or services that you can offer that the supplier may need.

Be Confident: Being confident in your negotiations can help you to get the best prices. Being confident in your ability to sell the products, as well as in your understanding of the market and the products, can give you an edge in negotiations.

Be Willing to Walk Away: Sometimes negotiations will not work out, and it's important to be willing to walk away from a deal that does not make sense for your business.

Build a Long-term Relationship: Building a long-term relationship with your supplier can also help you to negotiate better prices. By building a good relationship with your supplier, you may be able to negotiate better prices over time.

By taking the time to negotiate prices with suppliers, you can ensure that you are paying fair prices for the products you sell. It's important to remember that negotiating prices is not a one-time event, but an ongoing process. Prices can change based on market trends, demand, and other factors, so it's important to regularly review and renegotiate prices to ensure that they are still fair and profitable.

It's also important to have a clear communication with the supplier on how they handle shipping and customer service, and to have an understanding of the supplier's return policy. This can help to ensure that you are getting the best possible prices for the products, while also ensuring that you have a reliable and trustworthy supplier.

In addition, it's important to be aware of the supplier's minimum order quantities, as some suppliers may have a minimum order quantity required to maintain a profitable pricing. It's also important to negotiate payment terms, shipping costs and lead times.

Overall, negotiating prices with suppliers is a crucial step in building a successful drop shipping business. By researching wholesale prices, determining retail prices, and identifying your leverage, you can negotiate the best possible prices for the products you sell, increasing your profits and making it easier to grow your business.

Chapter two

Building Your Online Store

Building your online store is a critical step in establishing your drop shipping business. Your online store is the foundation of your business, and it's essential to create a store that is professional, easy to navigate, and visually appealing. This section will cover the following topics:

A. Platform Selection: The first step in building your online store is to select a platform. There are a variety of platforms available, such as Shopify, BigCommerce, and WooCommerce, each with its own set of features and benefits. It's important to choose a platform that fits your needs and is easy to use.

B. Design and Layout: The design and layout of your online store is crucial to its success. It's essential to create a design that is visually appealing, easy to navigate, and consistent with your branding. This includes choosing a color scheme, typography, and imagery that aligns with your brand identity.

C. Product Listing: Once the design and layout of your online store is in place, it's time to list your products. This includes creating product pages, writing product descriptions, and adding product images. It's important to ensure that the product information is accurate and up-to-date.

D. Payment and Shipping: Setting up payment and shipping options is an essential step in building your online store. This includes choosing a payment gateway, such as PayPal or Stripe, and setting up shipping rates and options. It's important to ensure that the checkout process is seamless and secure.

E. Marketing and Optimization: Once your online store is up and running, it's important to start marketing and optimizing it for search engines. This includes creating content, running ad campaigns, and optimizing your site for search engines.

By following these steps, you can build an online store that is professional, easy to navigate, and visually appealing. It's important to note that, building an online store is an ongoing process and it's essential to stay updated with market trends, customer demands, and technology to adapt accordingly.

Choosing the Right Platform

Choosing the right platform for your online store is an essential step in building your drop shipping business. There are a variety of platforms available, each with its own set of features and benefits. It's important to choose a platform that fits your needs and is easy to use.

Here are a few popular e-commerce platforms to consider:

Shopify: Shopify is one of the most popular e-commerce platforms, known for its ease of use, flexibility and scalability. It offers a wide range of features, including a drag-and-drop website builder, built-in success gateways, and a variety of apps and plugins to extend the functionality of your store.

BigCommerce: BigCommerce is another popular e-commerce platform that offers a wide range of features, including a built-in website builder, a variety of payment gateways, and integration with multiple sales channels. It also offers a wide range of customization options, allowing you to create a unique online store.

WooCommerce: WooCommerce is a free and open-source e-commerce platform, built on the WordPress platform. It offers a wide range of features, including a wide range of customization options and a variety of plugins to extend the functionality of your store.

Magento: Magento is an open-source e-commerce platform that is known for its scalability and flexibility. It offers a wide range of features, including a built-in website builder, a variety of payment gateways, and a wide range of customization options.

OpenCart: OpenCart is an open-source e-commerce platform that is known for its ease of use and simplicity. It offers a built-in website builder, a variety of payment gateways, and a wide range of customization options.

When choosing a platform, consider your technical skills and experience, budget, scalability and the features that are important for your store. It's also important to consider the support, documentation and community available for the platform.

It's important to choose a platform that is easy to use, offers the features you need, and is scalable to grow with your business. By choosing the right platform, you can ensure that your online store is professional, easy to navigate, and visually appealing.

Designing Your Store

Designing your online store is a crucial step in building your drop shipping business. The design and layout of your store can impact customer engagement, conversion rates, and overall sales. It's essential to create a design that is visually appealing, easy to navigate, and consistent with your branding.

Here are a few tips for designing your online store:

Branding: The design of your store should align with your brand identity. This includes choosing a color scheme, typography, and imagery that aligns with your brand. Your logo should be prominently displayed on your website.

Navigation: The navigation of your store should be easy to use, intuitive, and consistent across all pages. It's important to organize your products in a logical manner, and to make it easy for customers to find what they're looking for.

Visuals: High-quality images and videos can help to showcase your products, and make them more appealing to customers. It's important to use high-resolution images and videos that accurately represent your products.

Mobile-Responsive Design: With more and more customers shopping on their mobile devices, it's important to ensure that your store is optimized for mobile. This includes using a mobile-responsive design, and ensuring that your store loads quickly on mobile devices.

User Experience: The user experience of your store should be seamless, and the checkout process should be easy and secure. It's important to ensure that your store is easy to use, and that the checkout process is as simple as possible.

Test and Optimize: It's important to test and optimize your store to ensure that it is performing well. This includes testing the design, user experience, and checkout process, and making changes as needed.

By designing a visually appealing, easy to navigate, and user-friendly store, you can increase customer engagement, conversion rates, and overall sales. It's important to note that, designing an online store is an ongoing process and it's essential to stay updated with market trends, customer demands and design best practices to adapt accordingly.

Setting Up Payment and Shipping

Setting up payment and shipping options is an essential step in building your online store. This includes choosing a payment gateway, such as PayPal or Stripe, and setting up shipping rates and options. It's important to ensure that the checkout process is seamless and secure.

Here are a few tips for setting up payment and shipping options:

Payment Gateway: The first step in setting up payment options is to choose a payment gateway. A payment gateway is a service that processes online payments, and there are a variety of options available, such as PayPal, Stripe, and

Square. It's important to choose a payment gateway that is reliable, secure, and easy to use.

Shipping Options: Once you have set up your payment gateway, the next step is to set up shipping options. This includes determining shipping rates, creating shipping options, and setting up shipping methods. It's important to offer a variety of shipping options, such as standard, express, and international shipping.

Tax Settings: Setting up tax settings is also important. This includes determining the tax rates that apply to your products and setting up the appropriate tax settings in your online store.

Order Management: It's also important to set up an order management system to keep track of orders, process payments, and manage shipping. This can be done through your e-commerce platform or by using a third-party system.

Secure Checkout: Finally, it's important to ensure that the checkout process is secure. This includes using SSL certificates, and implementing security measures such as fraud detection and prevention.

By setting up payment and shipping options, you can ensure that your online store is ready to process payments and ship products. It's important to note that, setting up payment and shipping options is an ongoing process and it's essential to stay updated with market trends, customer demands, and shipping regulations to adapt accordingly.

Optimizing for Search Engines

Optimizing your online store for search engines is an important step in building your drop shipping business. By optimizing your store for search engines, you can increase visibility, drive more traffic, and boost sales. Here are a few tips for optimizing your online store for search engines:

Research Keywords: Researching keywords is the first step in optimizing your store for search engines. This includes identifying the keywords that your customers are using to find products similar to yours and incorporating them into your product titles, descriptions, and meta tags.

Optimize Product Pages: Optimizing your product pages is crucial for search engine optimization. This includes using keywords in the product title, description, and meta tags, as well as including high-quality images and videos.

Use Alt tags for images: Alt tags are a way to describe the images on your website. They help search engines understand the content of the images on your site and make it easier for customers to find your products.

Create Quality Content: Creating quality content is also important for search engine optimization. This includes writing product descriptions, blog posts, and creating videos that are informative and engaging.

Utilize social media: Utilizing social media is also an important aspect of search engine optimization. This includes creating a social media presence, sharing your products, and engaging with customers.

Monitor and Analyze: Finally, it's important to monitor and analyze your website's performance. Use tools like Google Analytics to track your website's traffic and conversion rate, and use the information to make data-driven decisions about how to optimize your site for search engines.

By following these tips, you can optimize your online store for search engines, increase visibility, drive more traffic, and boost sales. It's important to note that, optimizing for search engines is an ongoing process, and it's essential to stay updated with search engine algorithms and trends to adapt accordingly.

chapter three

Marketing and Advertising

Marketing and advertising are essential steps in building a successful drop shipping business. By marketing and advertising your products, you can increase visibility, drive more traffic, and boost sales. This section will cover the following topics:

A. Social Media Marketing: Utilizing social media platforms such as Facebook, Instagram, and Twitter can be an effective way to market and advertise your products. This includes creating a social media presence, sharing your products, and engaging with customers.

B. Influencer Marketing: Influencer marketing is a popular and effective way to market and advertise your products. This includes partnering with influencers in your niche to promote your products and reach a wider audience.

C. Email Marketing: Email marketing is another effective way to market and advertise your products. This includes sending regular newsletters, special promotions, and product updates to your email list.

D. Paid Advertising: Paid advertising, such as Google AdWords, Facebook ads, and Instagram ads, can be an effective way to reach a wider audience and drive more traffic to your store.

E. Content Marketing: Creating quality content, such as blog posts, videos, and infographics, can be an effective way to market and advertise your products. This includes creating informative and engaging content that provides value to your target audience.

F. Analyze and Optimize: It's important to analyze and optimize your marketing and advertising efforts. This includes monitoring the performance of your campaigns, analyzing data, and making data-driven decisions on how to improve your marketing and advertising strategies.

By implementing these marketing and advertising strategies, you can increase visibility, drive more traffic, and boost sales. It's important to note that, marketing and advertising is an ongoing process and it's essential to stay updated with market trends, customer demands, and technology to adapt accordingly.

Building Your Brand

Building a strong brand is an essential step in building a successful drop shipping business. A strong brand can help you to stand out in a crowded market, build customer loyalty, and increase sales. Here are a few tips for building your brand:

Define your brand: The first step in building your brand is to define it. This includes developing a brand strategy, creating a unique value proposition, and identifying your target audience.

Create a Brand Identity: Once you have defined your brand, the next step is to create a brand identity. This includes creating a logo, color scheme, typography, and imagery that aligns with your brand.

Develop a Brand Voice: Developing a brand voice is also important. This includes creating a tone of voice and messaging that aligns with your brand identity and resonates with your target audience.

Consistency: Consistency is key in building your brand. This includes ensuring that your branding is consistent across all platforms, including your website, social media, and advertising.

Communicate your brand: Communicating your brand is essential for building brand awareness. This includes sharing your brand story, promoting your unique value proposition, and engaging with your target audience.

Measure and Adapt: Building a brand is an ongoing process and it's important to measure and adapt your efforts. This includes monitoring your brand's performance, analyzing data, and making data-driven decisions on how to improve your branding efforts.

By following these tips, you can build a strong brand that helps you to stand out in a crowded market, build customer loyalty, and increase sales. It's important to note that, building a brand is an ongoing process and it's essential to stay updated with market trends, customer demands and technology to adapt accordingly.

Creating a Marketing Plan

Creating a marketing plan is an essential step in building a successful drop shipping business. A marketing plan outlines the strategies and tactics you will use to reach your target audience, increase visibility, and drive sales. Here are a few tips for creating a marketing plan:

Define your goals: The first step in creating a marketing plan is to define your goals. This includes identifying what you want to achieve with your marketing efforts, such as increasing website traffic, boosting sales, or building brand awareness.

Identify your target audience: Identifying your target audience is also an important step in creating a marketing plan. This includes understanding the demographics, psychographics, and behaviors of your target audience, as well as their needs and pain points.

Research your competition: Researching your competition is also important. This includes understanding their strengths and weaknesses, as well as identifying opportunities to differentiate your brand from theirs.

Create a budget: Creating a budget is an essential step in creating a marketing plan. This includes determining how much you can afford to spend on marketing efforts and allocating resources accordingly.

Develop a strategy: Developing a strategy is also important. This includes identifying the tactics and channels you will use to reach your target audience, such as social media, email marketing, or paid advertising.

Implement, Monitor and adjust: Implementing, monitoring and adjusting your marketing plan is also important. This includes implementing the tactics and channels you have identified, monitoring the performance of your efforts, and making data-driven decisions to improve your marketing plan.

By following these tips, you can create a marketing plan that helps you to reach your target audience, increase visibility, and drive sales. It's important to note that, creating a marketing plan is an ongoing process and it's essential to stay updated with market trends, customer demands, and technology to adapt accordingly.

Utilizing Social Media

Utilizing social media is an essential step in building a successful drop shipping business. Social media platforms, such as Facebook, Instagram, and Twitter, can be used to market and advertise your products, engage with your target audience, and build brand awareness. Here are a few tips for utilizing social media:

Identify the right platforms: The first step in utilizing social media is to identify the platforms that are most relevant to your target audience. This includes understanding the demographics, interests, and behaviors of your target audience, as well as the features of each platform.

Create a content calendar: Creating a content calendar is also important. This includes planning out the content you will post, such as product images, videos, and blog posts, as well as the timing of your posts.

Create engaging content: Creating engaging content is also important. This includes creating content that is informative, helpful, and provides value to your target audience.

Use paid advertising: Utilizing paid advertising on social media platforms, such as Facebook and Instagram, can be an effective way to reach a wider audience and drive more traffic to your store.

Engage with your audience: Engaging with your audience is also important. This includes responding to comments and messages, and creating a sense of community on your social media platforms.

Monitor and Analyze: Finally, it's important to monitor and analyze your social media efforts. This includes tracking the performance of your posts, analyzing data, and making data-driven decisions on how to improve your social media strategy.

By following these tips, you can utilize social media to market and advertise your products, engage with your target audience, and build brand awareness. It's important to note that, utilizing social media is an ongoing process and it's essential to stay updated with market trends, customer demands, and technology to adapt accordingly.

It's also important to note that, not all social media platforms will be relevant to your business, it's crucial to focus on the most relevant platforms that align with your target audience and product. When creating content, it's important to create a balance of promotional and non-promotional content, this will not only help you to build a loyal following, but it will also help you to establish your brand as an authority in your niche.

When using paid advertising, it's important to test different targeting options, ad formats and messaging to find the most effective way to reach your target audience. It's important to monitor your campaigns and track their performance using tools like Google Analytics, Facebook Insights, and Instagram Insights.

Finally, it's important to be consistent with your social media efforts. This means regularly posting new content, engaging with your audience, and monitoring your campaigns. By being consistent, you can build a loyal following, increase visibility, and drive more sales.

chapter four

Implementing Paid Advertising

Implementing paid advertising is an essential step in building a successful drop shipping business. Paid advertising, such as Google AdWords, Facebook ads, and Instagram ads, can be an effective way to reach a wider audience, drive more traffic to your store, and boost sales. This section will cover the following topics:

A. Setting up a campaign: The first step in implementing paid advertising is to set up a campaign. This includes identifying the platform you will use, such as Google AdWords or Facebook ads, and creating an account.

B. Targeting: Once you have set up your campaign, the next step is to target your audience. This includes identifying the demographics, interests, and behaviors of your target audience, as well as the keywords and phrases they are using to find products like yours.

C. Ad formats: Understanding different ad formats is also important. This includes text ads, image ads, video ads, carousel ads, and more. Each ad format has its own set of best practices and guidelines, it's important to choose the right one that aligns with your marketing objectives.

D. Creating Ads: Creating engaging and effective ads is also important. This includes using high-quality images, videos, and copy that aligns with your brand identity and resonates with your target audience.

E. Optimizing and testing: Optimizing and testing your ads is also important. This includes monitoring the performance of your ads, analyzing data, and making data-driven decisions on how to improve your ads.

F. Monitor and Analyze: Finally, it's important to monitor and analyze the performance of your campaigns. This includes tracking the performance of your ads, analyzing data, and making data-driven decisions on how to improve your campaigns.

By implementing paid advertising, you can reach a wider audience, drive more traffic to your store, and boost sales. It's important to note that, paid advertising is an ongoing process and it's essential to stay updated with market trends, customer demands, and technology to adapt accordingly.

Managing and Scaling Your Business

Managing and scaling your drop shipping business is an essential step in maintaining its success. This section will cover the following topics:

A. Inventory management: Inventory management is an important aspect of managing and scaling your business. This includes keeping track of your inventory levels, monitoring sales, and reordering products as needed.

B. Order fulfillment: Order fulfillment is also an important aspect of managing and scaling your business. This includes processing orders, managing shipping, and handling returns and refunds.

C. Financial management: Financial management is also an important aspect of managing and scaling your business. This includes keeping track of your revenues and expenses, creating financial reports, and making data-driven decisions on how to improve your business's financial performance.

D. Customer service: Providing excellent customer service is also an important aspect of managing and scaling your business. This includes responding to customer inquiries and complaints, addressing any issues that may arise, and working to build customer loyalty.

E. Automation: Automating certain tasks is also an important aspect of managing and scaling your business. This includes using tools and software to automate tasks such as inventory management, order fulfillment, and financial management.

F. Expansion and Diversification: As your business grows, it's important to consider expanding and diversifying your product offerings, exploring new market opportunities, and scaling your operations to meet the increased demand.

By effectively managing and scaling your business, you can maintain its success and continue to grow it over time. It's important to note that, managing and scaling your business is an ongoing process and it's essential to stay updated with market trends, customer demands, and technology to adapt accordingly.

Managing Inventory and Orders

Managing inventory and orders is an essential step in maintaining the success of your drop shipping business. Inventory management refers to keeping track of your inventory levels, monitoring sales, and reordering products as needed. Order fulfillment refers to the process of processing orders, managing shipping, and handling returns and refunds.

Here are a few tips for managing inventory and orders:

Keep track of your inventory levels: It's important to keep track of your inventory levels, this includes monitoring stock levels, noting which items are selling well and which are not, and reordering products as needed.

Set up a system for tracking orders: Setting up a system for tracking orders is also important. This includes using a software or a spreadsheet to keep track of orders, shipping information, and customer information.

Choose a reliable supplier: Choosing a reliable supplier is also important. This includes researching the supplier's reputation, their delivery times, and their return and refund policies.

Communicate with your customers: Communicating with your customers is also important. This includes providing them with tracking information, keeping them updated on their order status, and handling any issues that may arise.

Automate where possible: Automating certain tasks is also important. This includes using inventory management software, order processing software, and shipping software to automate tasks such as inventory management, order fulfillment, and shipping.

Monitor and Analyze: Finally, it's important to monitor and analyze your inventory and order management efforts. This includes tracking the performance of your inventory and order management, analyzing data, and making data-driven decisions on how to improve your inventory and order management.

By effectively managing your inventory and orders, you can ensure that your customers receive their products in a timely manner and that you're always able to fulfill their orders. It's important to note that, managing inventory and orders is an ongoing process and it's essential to stay updated with market trends, customer demands, and technology to adapt accordingly.

Handling customer service is an essential step in maintaining the success of your drop shipping business. Customer service refers to the process of responding to customer inquiries and complaints, addressing any issues that may arise, and working to build customer loyalty.

Here are a few tips for handling customer service:

Respond promptly: Responding promptly to customer inquiries and complaints is important. This includes answering customer questions, addressing any issues that may arise, and providing updates on the status of their orders.

Be professional and friendly: Being professional and friendly when communicating with customers is also important. This includes using a polite and helpful tone, providing clear and concise information, and showing empathy when addressing customer complaints.

Provide multiple channels for customer service: Providing multiple channels for customer service is also important. This includes offering email, phone, and live chat support, as well as a FAQ section on your website.

Resolve issues quickly: Resolving issues quickly is also important. This includes addressing customer complaints and concerns in a timely manner, and providing clear and detailed information on how the issue will be resolved.

Follow up with customers: Following up with customers is also important. This includes checking in with customers after an issue has been resolved to ensure that they are satisfied with the outcome, and also, it helps to identify areas for improvement.

Monitor and Analyze: Finally, it's important to monitor and analyze your customer service efforts. This includes tracking customer feedback, analyzing data, and making data-driven decisions on how to improve your customer service.

By effectively handling customer service, you can build customer loyalty, improve customer satisfaction, and ultimately drive more sales. It's important to note that, handling customer service is an ongoing process and it's essential to stay updated with market trends, customer demands, and technology to adapt accordingly.

Analyzing Data and Making Decisions

Analyzing data and making decisions is an essential step in maintaining the success of your drop shipping business. This process involves collecting, analyzing and interpreting data from various sources such as website analytics, customer feedback, and sales data, in order to make informed decisions that will improve your business performance.

Here are a few tips for analyzing data and making decisions:

Collect data from various sources: Collecting data from various sources is important. This includes website analytics, customer feedback, and sales data. The more data you have, the better equipped you will be to make informed decisions.

Use the right tools: Use the right tools to analyze your data. This includes using analytics software, such as Google Analytics, to track website traffic, conversion rates, and customer behavior.

Identify key performance indicators (KPIs): Identify key performance indicators (KPIs) that are important to your business. This includes metrics such as website traffic, conversion rates, customer acquisition costs, and customer lifetime value.

Analyze the data: Analyze the data to identify patterns and trends. This includes looking for patterns in customer behavior, identifying areas where your business is performing well and areas where it can improve.

Make data-driven decisions: Make data-driven decisions based on the insights you have gained from analyzing your data. This includes making decisions on how to improve your website, marketing efforts, and customer service.

Monitor and adapt: Finally, it's important to monitor your progress and adapt your strategy as needed. This includes tracking your progress against your KPIs, analyzing the results, and making data-driven decisions on how to improve your business performance.

By effectively analyzing data and making decisions, you can improve your business performance, increase efficiency, and ultimately drive more sales. It's important to note that, analyzing data and making decisions is an ongoing process and it's essential to stay updated with market trends, customer demands, and technology to adapt accordingly.

Scaling Your Business

Scaling your drop shipping business is the process of expanding and growing your business operations to meet increasing demand. As your business grows, it's important to consider expanding and diversifying your product offerings, exploring new market opportunities, and scaling your operations to meet the increased demand.

Here are a few tips for scaling your business:

Assess your current capacity: Before scaling your business, it's important to assess your current capacity. This includes evaluating your current resources, such as staff, equipment, and inventory, and determining if they are sufficient to meet increased demand.

Identify new market opportunities: Identifying new market opportunities is also important. This includes researching new niches, identifying new target audiences, and exploring new distribution channels.

Expand and diversify your product offerings: Expanding and diversifying your product offerings is also important. This includes introducing new products, experimenting with new product lines, and diversifying your product offerings to appeal to a wider range of customers.

Invest in automation: Investing in automation is also important. This includes using automation tools and software to streamline your operations, such as inventory management, order fulfillment, and shipping.

Hire and train additional staff: Hiring and training additional staff is also important. This includes recruiting and training new staff to handle increased demand, and ensuring that your staff have the necessary skills and knowledge to perform their jobs effectively.

Monitor and adapt: Finally, it's important to monitor your progress and adapt your strategy as needed. This includes tracking your progress against your business goals, analyzing the results, and making data-driven decisions on how to improve your business performance.

By effectively scaling your business, you can increase your revenue, improve your efficiency, and ultimately drive more sales. It's important to note that, scaling your business is an ongoing process and it's essential to stay updated with market trends, customer demands, and technology to adapt accordingly.

Conclusion

The conclusion of a book on drop shipping serves as a summary of the key takeaways from the book and an opportunity to leave the reader with a lasting impression.

In this book, we discussed the basics of drop shipping and how it can be a great way to start an online business. We also covered important aspects of starting a drop shipping business such as finding the right products, researching demand, identifying suppliers, evaluating quality, negotiating prices, building an online store, marketing and advertising, and managing and scaling the business.

We also delved into more specific topics such as implementing paid advertising, managing inventory and orders, handling customer service, and analyzing data and making decisions.

In conclusion, drop shipping can be a great opportunity for those looking to start an online business. With the right approach, you can find success in this space. However, it's important to remember that starting and running a business takes hard work, dedication, and perseverance. It's important to stay updated with the market trends, customer demands, and technology to adapt accordingly. The key takeaway from this book is that with the right approach, drop shipping can be a rewarding and profitable business venture.

The key takeaways from this book on drop shipping include:

Drop shipping can be a great way to start an online business: Drop shipping allows individuals to start an online business without having to invest in inventory upfront. It's a cost-effective way to start a business, and it allows for flexibility in terms of product offerings.

Finding the right products is crucial: Finding the right products to sell is crucial for the success of your drop shipping business. This includes researching demand, identifying suppliers, evaluating quality, and negotiating prices.

Building an online store is important: Building an online store is an important step in starting a drop shipping business. This includes choosing the right platform, designing your store, setting up payment and shipping, and optimizing for search engines.

Marketing and advertising is crucial: Marketing and advertising is crucial for the success of your drop shipping business. This includes building your brand, creating a marketing plan, and utilizing social media.

Managing and scaling your business is important: Managing and scaling your business is an essential step in maintaining its success. This includes inventory management, order fulfillment, financial management, customer service, automation, and expansion and diversification.

Analyzing data and making decisions is important: Analyzing data and making decisions is an essential step in maintaining the success of your drop shipping business. This includes collecting data from various sources, using the right tools, identifying key performance indicators, analyzing the data, making data-driven decisions, and monitoring and adapting your strategy.

It's important to remember that starting and running a business takes hard work, dedication, and perseverance. By following the key takeaways outlined in this book, you can increase your chances of success in the drop shipping business.

Additional Resources

In addition to the information provided in this book, there are many resources available to help you start and grow your drop shipping business. Here are a few suggestions:

Blogs and forums: There are many blogs and forums dedicated to drop shipping, e-commerce and online business. You can find a wealth of information, tips, and advice on these sites. Some popular blogs include: Oberlo, Shopify, SaleHoo

Online Courses: There are also many online courses available on drop shipping and e-commerce. These courses can provide you with more in-depth information and help you learn the skills you need to start and grow your business. Some popular online courses include: Ecom Elites, Drop Ship Lifestyle, Ecom Entrepreneurs.

Books: There are also many books available on drop shipping, e-commerce, and online business. Reading books on these topics can help you gain a deeper understanding of the industry and provide you with valuable insights and strategies.

Networking: Networking with other entrepreneurs in the e-commerce and drop shipping industry can be extremely valuable. You can learn from their experiences, gain valuable insights and make important connections that can help you grow your business.

Social media groups: Joining social media groups can also be helpful. You can learn from others and ask questions. They can be an excellent place to connect with other business owners, gain insights, and share experiences.

It's important to remember that starting a business takes time and effort, but with the right resources and support, you can increase your chances of success.

In conclusion, starting a drop shipping business can be a great way to start an online business without having to invest in inventory upfront. It's a cost-effective way to start a business and allows for flexibility in terms of product offerings. However, it's important to remember that starting and running a business takes hard work, dedication, and perseverance.

The key to success in drop shipping is finding the right products, building an online store, marketing and advertising, managing and scaling your business, and analyzing data and making decisions. It's important to stay updated with market trends, customer demands, and technology to adapt accordingly.

In this book, we discussed the basics of drop shipping and provided tips and strategies on how to start and grow a successful drop shipping business. We also provided resources that can help you learn more about drop shipping and e-commerce.

It's important to keep in mind that the road to success is not always easy, but with the right approach and the right resources, you can increase your chances of success. Remember to stay patient, stay dedicated, and keep learning. By following the key takeaways outlined in this book, you can increase your chances of success in the drop shipping business.

Appendix

Glossary of Key Terms:

Drop shipping: A fulfillment model where a store doesn't keep the products it sells in stock. Instead, when a store sells a product, it purchases the item from a third party and has it shipped directly to the customer.

Inventory management: The process of keeping track of inventory levels, monitoring sales, and reordering products as needed.

Order fulfillment: The process of processing orders, managing shipping, and handling returns and refunds.

Key performance indicators (KPIs): Metrics used to measure the performance of a business, such as website traffic, conversion rates, customer acquisition costs, and customer lifetime value.

Automation: The use of technology, such as software and tools, to streamline business operations.

B. List of Recommended Tools and Resources:

Shopify: A popular e-commerce platform that allows you to create an online store and manage your inventory and orders.

Oberlo: A Shopify app that allows you to easily import products from AliExpress and fulfill orders with just a few clicks.

Google Analytics: A free web analytics service that tracks and reports website traffic.

SEMrush: A digital marketing tool that helps you track your search engine rankings, analyze your competitors, and optimize your website for search engines.

MailChimp: An email marketing tool that allows you to create and send marketing campaigns to your email list.

Canva: A graphic design tool that allows you to create professional-looking designs for your website and marketing materials.

C. Sample Business Plan:

Executive Summary: A brief overview of your business, including your mission, goals, and target market.

Market Analysis: A detailed analysis of the market, including your target market, competitors, and industry trends.

Sales and Marketing Strategy: A plan for how you will reach your target market and generate sales.

Operations and Logistics: A plan for how you will manage your inventory, fulfill orders, and handle customer service.

Financial Projections: A forecast of your revenue, expenses, and profitability.

It's important to note that the sample business plan is just a sample and the actual business plan will depend on the specific business details and goals. It's always best to consult with professionals or experts in the field for a comprehensive and tailored business plan.

www.ingramcontent.com/pod-product-compliance
Lightning Source LLC
LaVergne TN
LVHW080818170826
845678LV00011B/2068
9798373894654